He Knew

A STORY ABOUT MY STRUGGLES, TRIALS AND TRIBULATIONS, AND WHERE GOD IS PREPARING ME TO GO.

TENESHA ROBINSON

Contents

—⊱❈⊰—

I have so many scars and I haven't been focused on them healing because all I do is hide behind them. I pray that this journey will show me that everything is part of God's plan whether it is good, bad or hurtful and that He will use it to push me closer to His vision and purpose for me getting me closer to the walk of becoming a Kingdom woman.

A Kingdom woman is who I am. A Kingdom woman is who God put me on this earth to be. He knew, but I didn't know. I have had many heartaches, so many struggles in life, but I made it through. Struggles still will come but with trust and faith, mountains can be moved. Many more mountains will need to be moved. I know this, because with God's grace and mercy they will continue to be moved... He knew and He knows!

God is so powerful to all and He wants me to lean on Him for understanding. I turned 44 this year, and God has shown me so many things including what He has in store for me. I just need to continue having faith because on this earth, man will let you down but God will never leave or forsake you.

I come from a strong praying family that believes in sticking together and loving one another through it all. We believe in putting God first. My parents and grandma raised me in such a blessed way. Looking back, I don't know how I would have made it without them, especially without the help of my grandma and the awesome God she serves.

She knew that God would make a way for me and my kids before He called her home.

My family has been through some tough times like any other, but we always know there will be sunshine. Every day, I feel my family's heart-filled love, and God loves to see His children love one another. My family rocks!

O Lord,

you have searched me [thoroughly]

and have known me.

Psalm 139:1(AMP)

Eventually, she took me to her aunt's house where I stayed for a couple of weeks. They fed me and treated me very well but still it was nothing like being with your family. Looking back though, I know that woman who took me in was my angel, sent by God to help me, protect me and get me in a safe place. Look how God sent that angel to me!

Everything happens for a reason. When you least expect it, He will make a way to get you through. He is a provider and a way maker. Oh Lord, thank you, thank you, thank you! I give you nothing but glory!

Though sometimes I don't feel strong enough at my age to handle the situations and obstacles that have come my way, God has spoken to me and shown me the way so many times and in so many ways.

God knows where He wants me and what He has in store for me, even though I still feel I'm not where I need to be in life. Trials and tribulations are just God's way of testing our faith. He is a way maker; He moves so many mountains and makes so many ways open to us because He knows what's best. God knows it all.

I pray for strength and peace because in this world today, we have to continue to lift one another up and not tear each other down. Sometimes I feel like I'm falling apart and am so alone. Sometimes I wonder what good praying will do, and if I can even pray at all because of how weak I feel at times. Even though in my weakness my faith allows me to look toward the hill, that glorious Calvary. I know and believe that God is here and that everything will be OK.

My faith reminds me that I serve a good God, a mighty good God, who knows and sees all. He has given and shown me grace and provides angels when I need them.

Proverbs tells us to lean on Him with all your heart and not your own understanding.

Trust in the Lord

with all thine heart;

and lean not unto

thine own understanding.

In all thy ways acknowledge him,

and he shall direct thy paths.

Proverbs 3:5-6 (KJV)

I want to continue to walk by faith and not by sight. God wants me to continue to trust Him with things I can't control. He wants me to lean on Him and Him alone.

God woke me up on my birthday this year at 5 in the morning. I felt His presence, and as I got on my knees to pray I kept hearing "Numbers 44" over and over. I finally got up to look in my Bible, but there isn't a Chapter 44 in the Book of Numbers, so I asked God what it was He was trying to tell me. I googled "biblically 44," and He told me: the biblical meaning of the number 44 is "chosen people/chosen one."

I begin to cry and pray, asking God if He was telling me that I'm one of the chosen ones. After that moment, I felt no pain, no hurt, and my whole day was filled with so much joy because I then knew that God has something for me...

but only in His time. I also know that 4+4=8, and 8 stands for new beginnings. That is what I am believing in and entrusting to Him, new beginnings!

God woke me up on several different mornings and placed these verses on my heart. I have been truly blessed by them.

You are now clean

of the word I have given to you.

John 15:3 (Contemporary English Version)

I do feel like I am being cleaned and renewed spiritually, because He has given me the truth and He does believe in me! I have to continue having faith and allow God to use me for my purpose He has for me to fufill!

Peace I leave with you,

my peace I give unto you:

not as the world giveth,

give I unto you.

Let not your heart be troubled,

neither let it be afraid.

John 14:27 (KJV)

I am thankful for the peace that He has given me and yes, I do believe that He wants me to have and know that peace is rest and not to worry or be afraid of anything. I will always trust that my God has me safe in His arms.

When Jesus

came down from the mountainside,

large crowds followed him.

A man with leprosy came

and knelt before him and said,

"Lord, if you are willing, you can make me clean."

Jesus reached out his hand

and touched the man.

"I am willing," he said.

"Be clean!"

Immediately, he was cleansed of his leprosy.

Matthew 8:1-3 (NIV)

I prayed one night for healing of my health and the pain I sometimes encounter. I prayed and asked God to take away the pain, and that morning this scripture came to me. I bowed down to God and prayed to feel better. He showed me that He healed the man with leprosy. God just wants us to obey, because He will provide all our needs. He will always make a way. Keep trusting and believing that He is a Healer.

O lord God of my salvation,

I have cried day and night before thee.

Let my prayer come before thee.

Let my prayer come before thee.

Incline thine ear unto my cry.

For my soul is full of troubles and

my life draweth nigh unto the grave.

Psalm 88:1-3 (KJV)

Days and nights, I've cried to God. I just didn't know what more I could ask of Him, if I could continue to ask Him to hear me. I didn't know what more to do, but it was time to pick myself up and know that troubles are not forever and to keep believing that joy will soon come in the morning.

A woman who fears the Lord

deserves to be praised.

Proverbs 1:30 (Amplified)

I am a woman who fears the Lord. I am a woman who wants to be obedient. I trust in Him with all my heart; I give Him nothing but praises because He has shown and given me so much grace! I will praise and honor Him at all times.

God

is

Sufficient

Understanding God's Goodness

When I was younger, I was in a bad car accident. It could have been worse than it was, but God looked after me and gave me another chance. Young and immature, I never even thought about God's goodness. But now I have an understanding of how good God is and how He works. I know how powerful God is and what He can do.

He kept me here for a reason. He knew I had a journey to live out. God is so much in the blessing business. Yes, I've been hiding behind the scars, but God will heal them if I allow Him to fill me up with the Holy Spirit. I want to feel the Holy Spirit in me every minute of every day; I want that feeling 24/7. I know if I trust Him and walk in faith, good things will happen.

ready to be changed in whatever way He wants to change me. I want to feel complete.

He has brought me out of so many storms and I know if I trust Him, He will make a way. He wants us to live by his laws, love our enemies and always remember that He forgives us. He is a great God who wants us to believe and endure in peace.

Let everyone see the light that shines on me. Jesus is my father! Through his grace, He can allow the people who have hurt me and even the ones I have hurt inside his house and into his presence. He knows the truth because He is the truth and the light. He is everything.

You know why? Because He knew! He knew and He knows the pain I've been through, the pain I'm enduring now and the pain I have yet to go through. I've made wrong turns and sometimes didn't know if I was turning left, right, up or down, but somehow God always showed me the right way to go. All I have to do is continue putting Him first and trusting and believing in Him! God is the potter and will continue to mold me into the vessel He put me on this earth to be.

Healing

---❧❧❧---

When I look and stare through the trees and up into the sky, I'm amazed by his creation and wonder how anyone could not believe. He is so amazing. He is everlasting life. I look back over my life, and it hits me just how good He's been to me. A single parent who worked job to job, from one unstable situation to another, I got away from knowing and respecting God the way I was raised. I did it all on my own but now, after all the distractions, the letdowns and the questionable decisions, I can do nothing but focus on Him and be so thankful in everything he has given and showed me. He is so worthy to be praised.

God believed in me even when it felt like no one else did. He blessed me with three beautiful children. Even in the face of hard times, my faith is strong and I know that He moves mountains and causes walls to fall. I know that as long as I can kneel before Him, I should be able to stand before anyone.

If God can make me stronger after a scare with my youngest child, He can make me stronger in any others. He healed my baby girl—my intelligent and beautiful baby girl—when she had gotten sick one night. She seemingly didn't have a breath left in her body, and I had reached the point where I felt the same way. I was so confused and in shock that I hung up on 911 and couldn't even think straight. I was panicking because I couldn't figure out what was wrong with her. But God stepped in and told me to listen to the 911 operator who was trying to help me. He made a way for my child to be well and safe. This was a test and a testimony, because my baby is a strong, gifted and talented little girl who God blessed to be on this earth to mold into His image.

He just wants us to stand and believe, to trust in his word and have faith! Getting through that storm helped me realize that He moves mountains. He will continue to guide and protect me, my family and loved ones. God knew and knows everything about me. He has forgiven me of my sins, of my disobedience. He is a forgiving God and wants us to be the same way, to live and love by his words.

He is Jehovah Jireh (my provider), Jehovah Nissi (my banner) and Jehovah Rapha (my healer). He will always be number one in my life. I am going to continue in this journey because I am determined to get to my destiny and fulfill my God's purpose for me. He wants me to keep walking in

His way and trusting His purpose for me. He wants me to thrive and not just survive, always keeping my Armor of God and hedge of protection around me at all times.

I always taught my kids that the first thing you should do when you wake up is thank God for waking you up and giving you another day. Even when my baby girl doesn't say it, sometimes she'll tell me, "Mommy, I forgot to tell God thank you for waking me up." I tell her that it's never too late to tell Him anything; He always hears you and loves you.